T0268875

On Corporate Governance

The Corporation As It Ought to Be

Michael Novak

The AEI Press

Publisher for the American Enterprise Institute

WASHINGTON, D.C.

1997

To order call toll free 1-800-462-6420 or 1-717-794-3800. For all other inquiries please contact the AEI Press, 1150 Seventeenth Street, N.W., Washington, D.C. 20036 or call 1-800-862-5801.

ISBN 978-0-8447-7082-6

1 3 5 7 9 10 8 6 4 2

The AEI Press
Publisher for the American Enterprise Institute
1150 17th Street, N.W., Washington, D.C. 20036

To the memory
of Michael A. Scully
(1949-1996),
who served his faith, his family,
his country, and his business vocation well,
and who was loved by his friends as
few men are.

Contents

Preface

In the summer of 1995, representatives of Pfizer
Inc. approached me about preparing three lectures on key issues facing business corporations
as the new century approaches. Although I was at
first hesitant to set aside a book project already begun, the freedom I had to choose topics and approach
led me to return to terrain I had first explored in the
1980s on the nature of the corporation in *The Corporation: A Theoretical Inquiry* and *Toward a Theology of the
Corporation.*

Much has changed in the intervening years. A
renewed account of the corporation seemed useful:
what the corporation is, its new moral challenges and
the new enemies it faces, and what goods (and dan-
gers) it brings with it. This monograph on corporate
governance is the third in a series of three Pfizer Lectures, the first two of which AEI recently published.

I would like to thank Pfizer Inc. for its sup-
port, and in particular Terry Gallagher and Carson
Daly. In my own office, Cathie Love and Brian Ander-
son carried on with their usual competence and unusual good cheer. Permit me to thank AEI, too, which
under the watchful eye of Chris DeMuth continues
to provide a remarkably welcome home for research
and writing; Isabel Ferguson and Ethel Dailey in the
office of seminars and conferences, who arranged the

public presentation on November 19, 1996; and Dana Lane, who showed her usual care in the supervision of this publication.

I would like to dedicate the published version of this lecture to Michael A. Scully, director of policy communications at Pfizer Inc., who died suddenly at the age of forty-seven on December 17, 1996. Mike and I had been colleagues in launching the well-regarded review *This World* (he was the editor) more than a decade ago, and I admired his quiet, shy ways and the passionate intellect they disguised more than words can say. I rejoiced at his marriage just a year and a half ago and at the birth of his daughter last spring. His friends and loved ones miss him deeply.

On Corporate Governance

L ike a proud frigate, the American business corporation is sailing confidently into the twenty-
first century. But a cannonade has already
erupted off port, and off starboard, rockets' red glare,
bombs bursting on "corporate governance" and "economic fairness." The corporation—the most successful institution of our time, flexible and adaptable beyond all others, maintaining its way in whitecapped
seas while others founder—is suddenly a ship that
others want to capture. They want to reform it into
something it is not. There is a lot of ruin in today's
cries for reforming corporate governance.[1]

Most of today's reformers are quite sophisticated.
They are no longer socialists, they say. They want to
"humanize" the corporation, not to expropriate it.
Some even quote a passage Adam Smith wrote about
the corporation in 1776, well before the nineteenth
century arrived. Smith feared that the corporation,
that then-new beast, slouching toward who knows
what city, that oddly contrived thing that separated
ownership from management, could not possibly

work. He gave three pretty good reasons why:

> The directors of such companies, being the managers rather of other people's money than their own, it cannot well be expected that they would watch over it with the same anxious vigilance with which the partners in a private copartnery frequently watch their own. Like the stewards of a rich man, they are apt to consider attention to small matters as not for their master's honour, and very easily give themselves a dispensation from having it. Negligence and profusion, therefore, must always prevail, more or less, in the management of the affairs of such a company. It is upon this account that joint stock companies for foreign trade have seldom been able to maintain the competition against private adventurers. They have, accordingly, very seldom succeeded without an exclusive privilege, and frequently have not succeeded with one. Without an exclusive privilege they have commonly mismanaged the trade. With an exclusive privilege they have both mismanaged and confined it.[2]

Adam Smith was analytically clear and prescient; the problems he described dog us still. But as a predictor of the corporation's future, he was uncharacteristically wrong.

Our strategy in attacking the subject of corporate governance is to resolve the question, What *is* the business corporation? and to follow through on its implications in today's unprecedented circumstances. This will require just over half the book. At the end, we need to tackle related problems such as the destructive power of envy, corporate compensation, and the corporate habit of appeasement.

What *Is* the Business Corporation?

Having been the social instrument by which the bourgeoisie, in "scarce one hundred years, has created more massive and more colossal productive forces than all preceding generations together," the publicly held business corporation is arguably the most successful, transformative, and future-oriented institution in the modern world.[3] It has been far more open, more creative, and infinitely less destructive than the nation-state, particularly the totalitarian state. Face to face with nation-states, churches have necessarily become their rivals, since in the moral sphere states lean to absolutism. But churches have not really had to become rivals to the corporation. For the corporation strives mightily to be compatible with every sort of religious regimen and not to challenge any frontally.

The corporation is by its nature a voluntary and part-time association, with no pretensions of being a total community (with rare exceptions, as in certain Japanese companies of a generation ago).[4]

Nonetheless, this fairly unassuming form of social organization has transformed the world before our eyes—thrown great silver airplanes into the skies, girdled the ether with invisible webs of instantaneous global communication, and brought fresh mangoes to the breakfast tables of the Northern Hemisphere and crisp, vacuum-packed Wheaties to the Southern. But what *is* a business corporation? It is so various a thing that it is not easy to define. In the United States, the publicly owned business corporation constitutes barely 1 percent of all business organizations. Unincorporated businesses, partnerships, small corporations, and even privately held giants (such as Mars, Inc., or Parsons Brinckerhoff, the huge engineering company) outnumber the publicly owned businesses 99 to 1. Yet this tiny minority of publicly owned firms produces more than half of America's economic output.

Moreover, publicly owned businesses come in all sizes and shapes, from networks of neighborhood hardware stores to manufacturers of millions of automobiles annually like General Motors and vast, sprawling energy companies like Mobil, Exxon, and Shell; from nimble, inventive cocoons of technical originality and marketing flair such as Intel and Microsoft, to the lumbering, but newly dynamic heirs of the nineteenth-century, night-whistling Atchison, Topeka & Santa Fe. You name it, you want it available to buy, and the likelihood is very great that a corporation is even now making it and looking for you.

So, what was the publicly owned business corporation invented to do? What is its purpose and point? What type of institution is it? By what standards ought it to be judged? These are crucial questions to resolve, before blindly careening into new forms of corporate governance.

Executive Energy

The great political philosopher Michael Oakeshott distinguished between two generically different types of association, the civic association and the enterprise association.[5] The civic association aims at something larger than any particular end, interest, or good: the protection of a body of general rules and a whole way of life; in other words, the larger framework within which, and only within which, the pursuit of particular ends becomes possible, peaceable, and fruitful. Given such a framework, individuals are free to choose myriad activities. The state is a civic association, he thought, or at least should be; so is the church; and so are many kinds of clubs, charitable organizations, and associations for self-improvement.

Oakeshott did not much like ideologically driven states, parties, or even activists; they narrow down the realm of choice. They falsify the nature and purpose of the state, making it a political party rather than a peaceable society.

By contrast, Oakeshott noted, the enterprise association is built to attain quite particular purposes, often purposes that tend to come around again quite continuously, as restaurants are built to feed people day after day. Enterprise associations are focused, purposive, instrumental, and executive: they fix a purpose and execute it.

Moral standards and standards of civic virtue still apply to enterprise associations, of course. "There is honor even among thieves," the ancient proverb says— but not enough! Enterprise associations that injure the virtue of their members—like states that injure virtue—

are objects of shame; consider the Mafia.

On other counts, however, publicly held business corporations are not at all like states, and their self-governance is not at all like that of a national government. These are two very different types of organization. In states, executive power is feared and therefore checked; in the corporation, it is desired and therefore husbanded. In this respect, in fact, corporate governance is perhaps a little like the executive branch of government taken by itself, apart from the judicial and the legislative branches. Like the executive branch, the governance of a business corporation requires a focused unity; there is little room within it for checks and balances.[6] Its point is executive, and "energy in the executive"[7] is its sine qua non. The corporation is not a state; its internal governance is not a state government—these are totally different species of association.

The standards of accountability to be met by the head of a major corporation are far narrower than those facing the head of the executive branch of government. His job description is very different from that of the president of the United States. The president must face democratic elections, itself an odd and not entirely executive measure of performance. The U.S. president must also play the almost kingly role of representing the people in symbol, rite, and performance.[8] Only in the third place does the president play the role of prime minister, that is, political strategist and persuader. Coming in a distant fourth is a U.S. president's role as executive officer of an administration, one of three branches of government. All this is very different from the president of Citicorp, who is selected by a small board and instructed to achieve defined objectives, within a relatively narrow strategic plan laid out by that same board (almost certainly with his input).[9]

Within a corporation, no one should even desire "separation of powers," for the whole point is to create something new, to achieve something, whereas in government the whole point is to prevent leaders from achieving anything beyond the already stated powers and purposes of the union. The reason for checks is to keep in check, and the reason for balances is to keep a balance. In an important sense, not achieving something, not violating the original constitution, is the preeminent aim. Wise persons do not want governments to act until they are carried forward, like rhinoceroses rising slowly from the mud, by the hydraulic force of a very large and durable consensus. But the same wise persons want business corporations to be able to act quickly, even to turn on a dime when they are losing money or when they spot suddenly arising possibilities, to take the risks for which their investors have entrusted them with well-defined executive power.

To repeat, governments move, must move, by consensus—slow as elephants and resistant as donkeys. But businesses must move by executive intention. Without waiting for public consensus—indeed, hoping to be first to reach the market—businesses must move instantly, like pulsing electronic signals. Often they must move by executive will, ready to act even before all the information is available that the intellect might crave.

Investors rightly want business to be effective;

they are willing to accept intuition, hunch, and even
instinct rather than the qualities they might prefer in
other contexts, such as full deliberation and judicious-
ness, so long as swift action results in more reliable
and speedier contact with reality than reflection. The
laws of action are not identical with the laws of reflection, and temperaments fitted to the one are not
always suitable for the other.

I linger on this point for one reason only. The
word *governance* naturally leads the mind to think of
government. Therefore, discussions of corporate governance tend to be conducted, often unconsciously,
in the language of political philosophy, worked out
for the government of nations. Such discussions lead
to an enormous mistake of logic and language, to a
way of thinking not at all appropriate for the governance of business corporations. The problem of business governance is not a problem of political philosophy; it is a problem of business philosophy. (In a similar way, theologians wince when they hear the governance of churches discussed in the language of political philosophy.) Politicians, churchmen, and people
in business ask different types of questions, work
under certain different rules, and require different
types of outcomes; even their manners and styles are
different. The general rule is this: for each different
type of human activity, its own proper philosophy.[10]

The problem, as Peter Drucker has suggested, is
that the philosophy of business is a field waiting to
be born. Indeed, Drucker himself tends to speak of
"organizational theory,"[11] which sounds a little like
sociology rather than a philosophy of business. What

we need is in fact a philosophy of business, because it is important to keep clear about what a business is and is not, especially today.

For the American business corporation has been so successful during the past hundred years, particularly during the past fifteen, that many people want to lasso it, break its spirit, and for their own purposes train it to become something else. Charities and helping organizations, for example, want the corporations to pay their upkeep. Heavily indebted and failed welfare states want to bend the corporation to meet the state's own unkept promises. In general, former socialists want to tame the business corporation, make it sit up and dance, perhaps do tricks to music.

As a matter of fact, after the dramatic collapse of the world's leading example of actually existing socialism, the USSR, socialists (and, in America, just plain "progressives"), without ever admitting their errors or correcting their way of thinking, still want to socialize the corporations. But now they want to do it through movements such as environmentalism, the philosophy of "stakeholders,"[12] children's rights,[13] and some forms of feminism and gay rights. And many corporate leaders are still being rolled, played for patsies, and driven forward blindly by their inability to think clearly and make distinctions.[14] Although appeasement seems to be an all-too-common reflex,[15] intellectual cowardice is not strictly required for business success. A sound philosophy is permitted. It must be developed, fortified, and honed to a practical edge not just by philosophers but by corporate doers themselves.

The Ant and the Elephant

What, then, is a business corporation, philosophically considered? From a philosophical point of view, the business corporation is so flexible, practical, polymorphous, adaptable, and various that no organizational definition of its essence is realistic. Most often, the corporation begins with an idea—an invention, perhaps, or simply an insight—around which investors pool their resources with the hope of creating new wealth.[16] But ideas for how to provide new goods or services are virtually infinite in shape and form. A part of a new corporation's originating idea, in fact, may be the conception of a new way of organizing the delivery of goods or services. Gateway Computers and Lands' End are not organized like Hewlett-Packard or Lord & Taylor. Pfizer is not organized like Rexall.

Furthermore, it is a mistake to think that only corporate executives at the large public firms are among the "rich" so widely disdained, at least in public, by leftist congressional and media leaders. The owner of the Ourisman auto dealerships in the Washington area, the retailer, may be wealthier than any executive at General Motors, the manufacturer. Ownership is, typically, a surer road to wealth than employment.

The concept of the business corporation, therefore, is like the magical ocean in the fairy tale, shallow enough for an ant to wade through and deep enough for an elephant to drown in. It must be as pluriform as the goods and services to be provided and the markets in which customers meet providers.

It must be able to change with changing times, technologies, political conditions, and moral habits. Its range is not infinite; there are cultures in which it cannot survive and others in which it cannot thrive.[17]

When, under Soviet communism, for instance, economic acts between consenting adults were punishable by death, in effect the private business corporation was in intensive care or dead. Circa 1979, on most of the territory of this planet (China, the USSR, and over other large geographical stretches) private corporations were *verboten*, forbidden, against the law. In many third world countries, epidemics of corruption and dictatorship—like plagues of leeches—bled corporations white and drove many of them out. In short, the corporation is a form of organization that can survive in most sorts of cultures but not in all.

In Adam Smith's day, the business enterprise was essentially a small owner-managed affair. As late as 1820, in all of France there were not more than several dozen business enterprises (or factories) employing as many as twenty persons in one building.[18] As Smith foresaw, the device of splitting ownership from management required by the growth of great stock associations shifted the flows of motives, interests, and passions.[19] When the executive manager was no longer the owner, he was in charge of spending someone else's money. (His compensation may be chiefly in stock ownership, but that does not make him *the* owner—far from it.) He might well feel comfortable with a handsome salary and enjoy the prestige of being boss, while losing the singular mark of the original owner—the willingness to be imaginative and take risks. The original owner, meanwhile, might have qualms about risks taken with his money by new managers, more qualms than he once had about risks he used to take lightheartedly for himself. As a thinker who paid a great deal of attention to men's passions, interests, and motives, Smith may have been the first to worry about future problems of corporate governance. He was not the last.

Why Do Firms Exist?

Why, then, despite Adam Smith's foreboding, do business corporations exist at all? (It once seemed to me that worrying about the existence of God was enough for a theologian, without worrying about the existence of firms.) There are two main reasons why firms exist, first pointed out by R. H. Coase in 1938 in a brilliant gem of an essay, "The Nature of the Firm,"[20] followed by a legion of other commentators including, recently, Richard Posner.[21] First, it may be far more efficient for an economic agent to hire many of the people his extensive activities will involve than to negotiate arms-length contracts with each of them as independent customers or suppliers. Such negotiations would otherwise consume his energies and time, and make day-to-day adjustments nearly impossible.[22] Second, in manufacturing, for instance, the need for capital is immense. Organizing a firm to rationalize, focus, and synchronize diverse economic activities is the most efficient way to attract capital.

    In our day, therefore, at least this much can be said in defining the business corporation: it is an enterprise association that depends on the public market for investors willing to invest a portion of their savings in it. It is legally incorporated as a legal person and governed under by-laws and by a duly appointed or elected board of directors. Its purpose is to provide goods and services of a distinctive type (or in a distinctive way) in the expectation of earning profits for its investors, with fiduciary care for the investments entrusted to it. It is the most efficient way yet discovered to minimize transaction costs and attract large amounts of investment capital. The corporation so conceived is the world's best hope for the creation of new economic wealth.

Pirates!

In the 1980s, financiers like Carl Icahn, Michael Milken, and many others began to make an analysis of the problems of corporate organization not unlike that of Adam Smith. They judged that many corporate managers were not doing nearly as well as they could with the value under their stewardship. Armed with new financial methods of their own devising for assembling large amounts of capital, they began buying and reshaping corporations to bring out overlooked values. No good deed going unpunished, these laser-eyed analysts were treated like pirates preying on Spanish galleons that had gold hidden in their holds. "Corporate raiders" they were called—and worse—and they terrorized an entire ocean of slowly moving companies.

Alarmed and awakened, corporate executives and corporate boards began trimming ship and preparing either to repel the Blackbeards or to outsail them. Disapprove of them or not, we owe these "pi-

rates" a debt. They were not alone in issuing a stir-
ring wake-up call—worldwide economic competition
arrived simultaneously—but they certainly got
everyone's attention.[23]

And they left us with a lingering problem. What
if corporate management *is* comfortable and content
with "good enough"—or worse? What should be
done, and who should do it? All may agree that corporate managers are not the most important owners,
only somewhat more so than mere employees—for,
even as employees, most of their compensation comes
as stock ownership, much of it in options that give
them longer-term interests than many ordinary stockholders. But, insofar as they are employees, who is it
that really employs them? Legally, it is the board of
directors that has that responsibility, along with several other responsibilities, such as the strategic direction of the company and provident forethought about
its resources, needs, and future contingencies. But
what if the board is in the pocket of, or in collusion
with, the corporate managers, some of whom also sit
on the board? What if the board loses dispassionate
objective distance? Critics have by now developed
several lines of assault.[24]

Besides, who *are* the owners of the contemporary corporation? Who are they in whose name the
board of directors acts as steward? In a publicly
owned company, the rightful owners may be scattered
all over the stock market. More likely, though, large
portions of the shares of any major company are held
by specific mutual funds, pension plans, and other
institutional investors, acting as proxies for hundreds
of thousands of individual owners, most of whom

are likely to be, in the term of art, *rationally ignorant*—
that is, poorly informed and willingly uninvolved—
concerning an individual corporation's practices and
prospects.[25]

Mutual Funds and Pension Funds

In fact, two great changes in the structure of corporate ownership have transformed the environment in
which corporations now operate. First, mutual funds
today are far more numerous than they were fifty
years ago. Second, by now the pension plans of employees, not only private but also public, own nearly
30 percent of the stock of major corporations.[26] All by
itself, the pension plan of the California State Public
Employees owned $72 billion in assets in 1993, more
than the gross domestic product of some member
states of the United Nations.[27]

Both the directors of mutual funds and the directors of pension plans want to invest in corporations that produce high returns. They are competing
against their peers in seeking higher returns; they
demand "performance." Managers of corporations
that "perform" admirably year after year become
market favorites. As their corporations attract investors, the wealth of their stockholders increases. So
does the value of their own employees' pension plans
and the value of other pension plans invested in company stock, as does the value of the mutual funds that
have selected them for investment.

Thus, when someone writes or says that Wall
Street likes or does not like a particular company, we
need to remind ourselves that the active intelligence

that first reaches such judgments is probably work-
ing in a pension plan office in Sacramento or Albany
or Eugene, Oregon, or in a new, quick-to-the-draw
mutual fund in Denver, Santa Fe, or Fort Lauderdale,
or in the small and unpretentious offices of financial
legends in Menlo Park or Omaha. Wall Street has been
decentralized. One result is that corporate managers
dare not become lazy and self-satisfied. They have
powerful incentives to seek out untapped resources
within their own companies and to turn these to creative use. Money managers all around the country
are watching them like hawks, competing with one
another to spot hidden strengths or weaknesses before others do.

Moreover, the directors of pension plan funds
and other investors have learned by experience that
they can, if necessary, vote a chief executive officer
out of office by taking over the board of directors of
his corporation. They have already done so at GM,
American Express, IBM, and Westinghouse. Boards
have power to hire and fire, and boards are themselves elected (usually for renewable three-year
terms) by stockholders. Large stockholders cast
weighty votes. So large stockholders from pension
plans and mutual funds have begun throwing their
weight around. (When the directors of state pension
plans and mutual funds enter a room, corporate executives have learned what to call them—Ma'am or
Sir.)

Looking for the Right Stuff

Conversely, money managers are learning the hard
way that their bread is buttered by corporate manag-

ers with vision, steadiness, talent, and guts—in short, with what used to be called "the right stuff." That means character, wedded to a precise talent, a talent for figuring out the right thing to do and for doing it the right way and at the right time. Today there are a lot of people competing fiercely to find the few persons in the whole world not only capable of being great CEOs but already in place in the right companies. Corporations are executive enterprises. That is of their essence. In business, the quality of the people in charge determines nearly everything else.

On the brink of the twenty-first century, therefore, the environment within which corporate governance operates is drastically different from what it was even twenty years ago. The performance of CEOs is under much greater scrutiny. Investment flows are instantaneous and worldwide. Moving beyond traditional watchdogs of business such as banks and regulatory agencies, money managers at newly powerful institutions such as mutual funds and pension funds have gained an upper hand over corporate managers through computer-driven tools of analysis and boldly employed voting clout. Today every corporate manager in his right mind knows that his perch is insecure. Unless he is employed by a firm that he himself or his family founded (and not even that will always protect him), he can expect the average length of his tenure to be about that of a linebacker in the National Football League, a little less than six years. He faces very little danger from boredom, laziness, or complacency. What Learned Hand in the 1950s called in a famous monopoly case "the quiet life" is no longer the CEO's lot. He will be lucky to have the

freedom of spirit to make time for solitude and soul.
He will be lucky not to make a mess of his family
relationships, especially with spouse and older children.

A Well-lighted Place

To summarize the argument thus far: once you grasp
the need for energy in the executive and note the new
competitive conditions prevailing in the corporate environment, much of the hullabaloo about corporate governance seems radically misplaced. According to most
of the analysis, the problem is that of finding checks
and balances and otherwise borrowing from the power-
limiting institutions of republican government. But the
problem of corporate governance is not to check
power—that is already done today by unprecedented
dimensions of competition—but rather to summon up
and channel power. Checks enough abound: the explo-
sion of financial information and analysis—not only in
the number of financial television channels, the Internet,
and the proliferation of financial newsletters but also in
the institutional power of independent professional
analysts representing large shareholders—has made the
business corporation quite suddenly a well-lighted
place.

Thus, what Adam Smith feared about the stock
association—that in zeal its managers would be infe-
rior to its owners—is not likely to happen today. In
fact, today's publicly owned firms run by hired managers may be far more performance oriented than
privately owned and managed firms of yesteryear.
There are now many more ways to keep chief execu-

tive officers on their toes than there were two decades ago. Investor checks and balances are very strong, indeed.

The great problem of corporate governance today, therefore, is not how to create checks and balances against power. The great problem is how to govern corporations internally to overcome the great cultural tide of envy and "political correctness" that bids fair to swamp them in syrupy, corrosive sentiment.

On Envy: "Thou Shalt Not Covet"

We turn, then, to the perennial and persistent problem of envy and its destructive social power, as well as to auxiliary problems such as corporate compensation and the strategy of appeasement.

Covetousness and envy are permanent and universal passions whose social destructiveness was recognized many civilizations ago, in the time of Deuteronomy, long before there were any business corporations. Universal covetousness and envy are burning embers that never die. Gasoline is thrown upon them today by such lines as these: "Executive compensation is obscene," "Corporate executives live too high," and "Wages of workers decline, while those of top management are growing astronomically." Not much is left for traditional socialists to do today except to fan prairie fires of covetousness and forest fires of envy.

Inequality is the main line of attack because "downsizing," last season's craze in the perpetual assault on corporations, turned out to be exaggerated.

Contrary to the impression fostered by the popular media, job stability has been slightly greater in recent years than in earlier periods.[28] The proportion of high-paying jobs has also been dramatically increasing, not decreasing. The corporations listed in the Fortune 500 have fewer employees today than twenty years ago, but a flood of smaller, newer high-tech companies has created a large labor market in high-skilled jobs.

It is quite true, if ironic, that Wall Street responds favorably to notice that behemoths like AT&T are re-structuring their work force. Announcements of lay-offs are sometimes met by small jumps in the stock price—sometimes, but not always. What do these positive effects mean? They mean that firms must meet the demands of new technologies and new worldwide competition. It means, further, that there is more value in AT&T than AT&T was previously delivering. (Recall that unrealized value belongs to the pension plans of millions of workers outside AT&T.) Change at AT&T was "overdue." The envi-ronment for laid-off workers with skills in communi-cations, luckily, is an up market.[29] Two-thirds of those laid off by AT&T were back at work in three months. With severance, some had, in effect, a paid vacation.

Let us return for a moment to the point that change was overdue. On a recent trip to Chile, a dis-tinguished business leader asked me why American firms wait so long before facing serious problems and then do so in a way so inhuman to their work force. Sometimes, of course, sudden technological change catches firms by surprise. But often, as silently as plaque on teeth, problems are building up even while executives neglect preventive measures. "Overdue change" is usually due to inadequate and tardy "executive energy," not to excessive energy. Much human turmoil might be spared if, on a regular basis, executives summoned up the energy to take countermeasures against inertial growth; preplanned attrition alone might do it.

Isn't it an irony, meanwhile, that leftist journalists and social critics, while becoming ever more skeptical about the desirability of the permanent marriage contract, should expect jobs to be forever? Do they expect employees to receive diamond rings on the day they are hired? In reality, finding good employees and training them is expensive, and mutual loyalty between firm and worker usually helps both. Under sudden layoffs, both suffer.

Incidentally, the fact that accusations about big corporations' "destroying jobs" occur at a time when the U.S. economy has created more than 50 million new jobs (during the past twenty-five years, at a rate of 19 million per decade) is not as paradoxical as it seems. In normal times, big firms are constantly reorganizing as conditions change; sometimes they shed jobs and sometimes they hire steadily. Some creation of new jobs—especially in entire industries never heard of before, such as among new technology companies—takes place in small firms (which by definition virtually all new firms are). And it is precisely by creating many new jobs that small firms become large firms. Many if not most small firms, however, are either suppliers or distributors for, or provide services to, large corporations.[30] The upshot is that a huge proportion of the U.S. labor force flocks like seagulls around the busy places generated by large, complex business organizations, no matter whether those businesses are hiring or shedding.

Two Types of Inequality

Still, the problem of inequality is a serious one, even if a false one. It is a false problem because there is and can be no human system that makes humans equal (in the sense of uniform). It is contrary to human nature even to *wish* to be considered identical to anyone else, replaceable, a cog in a slot. Individuals know they are unique, utterly unlike every other—quite unlike even their twin, if they happen to have one. They have unique ambitions, energy levels, moral strengths, knacks, and luck. Uniqueness, not uniformity, is the human mark.

Equality as uniformity, furthermore, can be socially imposed only through the most vigorous tyranny. The proper name for such a project is not egalitarianism but *egalityranny*. This project, in effect, lops off heads, slices off feet, and reduces the length of arms and fingers to a standard size. As such, equality-as-uniformity is antihuman. It is quite different from equality-as-uniqueness, which demands equal respect precisely for what is unequal (not uniform) in individuals.

This common-sense observation collides with two persistent facts. One is the universality of the human passions of envy, covetousness, and the desire to cut one's betters down. The other is that, in any democracy, many people resent the flaunting of differences of station, as if these represent a lapse into aristocratic privileges, a violation of democratic sensibilities. Both these facts—universal envy and democratic resentment—feed the boa constrictor that squeezes "equality" into "uniformity."

Unthinkingly, the flaunting of class differences does at times emanate from corporate board rooms, corporate parking places, corporate dining rooms, corporate jets, and other indiscreetly managed corporate perks. This is a serious fault. In democracies, corporations need to practice an unpretentious, open, man-in-the-street style at every level of the firm, or else they will awaken resentments in a democratic populace.[31]

Obviously, two further tendencies pull firms in opposite directions. Certain signs of status are inevitable, expected, and socially beneficial. Others are not. Some forms of recognition are offered in lieu of a raise. In any sound organization, superior achievement should receive superior recognition, and symbolic forms of recognition seem relatively costless. The trick, however, is not to allow differences in class status to arise between management and workers. This subject deserves often-renewed attention, for as marketing and sales departments well know, status pleases more than money, is eagerly sought and greedily devoured.

Nonetheless, wrongly signaled status is socially destructive. You cannot build community, teamwork, or a sense of family across fissures of rigid class consciousness. Ordinary folks want to believe that all class boundaries are permeable, if not by themselves, then in the person of their bright sons and daughters. The corporation needs to convey the air of being upwardly open. Alas, some corporate board rooms seem

designed to impress, to exclude, perhaps even to ex-
ude a hint of the baronial. I do not say that this is
always wrong; but it is, unless countered in other
ways, a great danger to the system as a whole.

For the moment Americans begin to think that
class lines are being drawn, bile rises in their bellies.
Management and labor need to share a similar world
of upward mobility, of achievable status, of belong-
ing to the same team. They must do so in fact, and
they must appear to do so. The tendency to forget
this—among union leaders, as well as managers—is
universal and perennial, so it must be consciously
combated. (Union leaders also face special tempta-
tions: to become confrontational in order to be viewed
as "fighters" for their members.) In a democracy, an
upwardly mobile, achievement-oriented, shared, and
open atmosphere inside the corporation is, I believe,
more important than the compensation levels of chief
executives.

Justifying Unequal Compensation

When salaries are moving upward throughout the
corporation, most Americans do not envy those
whose achievement and position entail higher salaries than their own; these are what they aspire to
achieve themselves. They want a ladder with rungs.
Americans resent uniformity. They are performance
oriented. For unequal performance, they want unequal pay.

When this general acceptance of understandable
inequalities breaks down, sound practice suggests
that it is best to look sharply at what is happening in

the bottom ranks. Salaries on different levels of an organization should generally rise and fall together. If most people's salaries are going up, practically everybody will be contented. But if salaries at the top keep rising rapidly while those at the bottom fall, stagnate, or rise only slightly, you can be certain feelings of unfairness will arise.

From ancient to modern times, the green worm of envy has been the chief and most regular destroyer of republican experiments: the envy that poisons the innards of one class, section, dynasty, family, or peer against another. Of course, envy never travels under its own name; it is the one vice that never calls itself what it is; it prefers prettier names, good names to which it has no right: "justice," "fairness," and the like. Companies should do everything in their power to defeat envy in every sphere they touch. No vice tears apart democracies more swiftly.

On corporate compensation, therefore, I would make two suggestions. First, one criterion of whether and how annual bonuses should be given—not the only criterion, but an important one—should include consideration of how lower-paid employees are being compensated. At the very least, the direction of compensation levels should be comparable: all should go up, down, or stagnate together, unless clear reasons can be cited for making exceptions in special cases. It may be that in certain crises more is asked of some employees than others, and for this they should be commensurately rewarded, for publicly defended reasons. Also, since half or more of senior executive pay comes by way of bonuses, in years when bonuses are canceled, contractual wages of workers may go up when wages of top executives go down; and that may be fair enough.

Some consideration should also be given to general wage levels outside the corporation. Corporate compensation levels are social facts of great significance in democracies, and they can no longer be hidden. Their public effect must be accounted for in advance. Reasons why they are set where they are set should always be offered to the public, with due forethought given to the public's probable reaction.

Second, for top executives, special new procedures must be designed to protect the neutrality, objectivity, and detachment of those who decide compensation levels, in the full glare of today's communications realities. At present, as the economist Irwin Stelzer has shown,[32] there are too many reasons to suspect lack of sufficient distance between those who serve on compensation committees and those they reward. From an ethical point of view, the real issue is not how much a particular CEO is paid, but by whom, using what methods, according to which criteria, and for what publicly defensible reasons. If an objective case may be made, the social effect is healthy; if the decision reeks of favoritism, the social effect is damaging to the business system as a whole and to democracy.

In such circumstances, envy is certain to uncoil from its slumbers and begin to slither through the body politic. Left-wing politicians feed on envy, but of course do not call it that; they say *compassion*. Envy is distinguished from compassion by a simple test: compassion rejoices in raising up the poor; envy rejoices in pulling down the rich. More than they admit, leftists love to see the rich and powerful humbled.

Against Appeasement

Argument over *governance* is often designed to avoid the main subject: *governors*. Since the point of business is to get things done, argument over governance must not be allowed to suggest the opposite of action—restraint on action or, even worse, process of the sort that pours molasses into the machinery. Reforms of governance must protect sufficient energy in the executive. This freedom to act, in turn, poses new tests for executives in our generation.

Oversight, collective consultation, information gathering, and some division of responsibility—these will always be needed, for reasons rooted in human ignorance, partiality, passion, and fallibility. Intelligent executives, therefore, may well decentralize decision making and rely on decision teams rather than solely on themselves. Their paramount concern is to be in constant touch with reality, and this requires as many eyes and ears, as many dispersed agents of practical wisdom, as possible. But the point of these safeguards is to protect the purposiveness of the corporation. Any scheme of governance that sinks executives in two feet of peanut butter violates the nature of executive institutions: *Executives must be allowed to execute.* They must be helped, strengthened, fully informed, corrected, and reinforced; but, in the end, they must be propelled to step forward to create new wealth.

Furthermore, it is wrong today for executives to conceive of their job narrowly, merely in its business aspects, without attention to its political setting and, even

more so, to its setting in the world of ideas. Bold in
business judgment, executives must not be pusillani-
mous in politics and mousy in the field of ideas. Let me
allude to a recent, and in some ways splendid, report
on corporate governance.[33] After reviewing all the powerful voices demanding change in corporate governance,
the author, a recently retired CEO, uncharacteristically
for him counsels a strategy of appeasement, by way of
a preemptive strike. That note of appeasement is the
glaring defect in an otherwise excellent analysis.

When reformers demand that corporations become more "responsible," the author rightly notes,
they mean *dedicated to causes dear to statists*, such as:
executive pay caps, incentives and mandates to cover
training and layoffs, constraints on internationaliza-
tion, demands for a Germanic system of "public interest" corporate directors, and other moves toward
the "socialization of corporate America." Before government mandates such things, however, the author
argues, businesses should preemptively set out a
menu of reforms. His recommendations: broaden
stock-option participation to unite the investment interests of workers with those of the corporation, open
up paths of decentralized entrepreneurship for employees, and go public against the excessive regula-
tion and unwise social mandates foisted on corporations. These are good suggestions.

Only two things are wrong. First, the author
marches them forward under the flag of appeasement:
they will punish us less if we punish ourselves first.
Second, the former corporate leader magnifies the
forces arrayed against corporations in politics and
public opinion and fails to summon up the full

strength of the intellectual case that corporate leaders can today make to the public.

In the past, preemptive strikes to appease the
ferocity of self-assured critics may have been necessary, even the best available response. But in today's
very different situation, corporate executives have a
new menu of responsibilities. In the economic arena,
rather than merely reacting to issues defined by the
Left, corporate executives need to set the terms for
the national political agenda and to frame public opinion early.

Everyone sees the need for economic growth,
even socialists. At their best, however, many executives are still reacting two years too late to issues
framed and organized by the Left long before. Much
too often, their highest aim is damage limitation. In
the arena of public opinion and public policy, tigers
in competition have appeared before the public as
lambs, bleating in appeasement.

This appeasement has taken two forms: first, intellectual and, second, programs of charitable giving.[34]
For some reason, many executives seem defensive
about the crucial value of capitalism, business, and
corporations to democracy. Knowing that many in the
press, the academy, left-wing politics, and political
activism are hostile to business and ardent support-
ers of the party of government, they seem to imagine
themselves in a no-win situation; the only question is
how much they will lose.

Appeasement seems to them the least harmful
solution. Indeed, some critics suggest that people in
business secretly feel guilty for becoming wealthy and
even enjoy being beaten up in the public eye. I do not

believe that, but it is a common theory.

To add insult to injury, these same executives often do, in fact, permit their corporate giving officers to reward with substantial grants the very activists who have advanced legislative agendas aimed at bringing corporate decisions under government control, inch by inch. Such executives no longer sell their enemies the rope by which they will be hanged; they give it to them as a grant.

In the past, such capitulation may have seemed the lesser evil. But now the fading night of the socialist empire, the darkening crisis of the welfare state, and the sepia image of the State as Beneficent Great Provider are yielding to bright Alpine sunlight. Our current intellectual situation is a new spring. Business leaders should study these changes, come abreast of them, and master the new viewpoint they afford.

A Cheerful View at the End of a Sorry Century

The overpromising state of the twentieth century has underachieved, its coffers are bare, and the unintended consequences of its overreaching are disheartening: a pronounced decline in morals and morale, a growing underclass, and a return to serfdom. But look at the contrast: the inventiveness of U.S. corporations and the tough-minded ways in which executives have reshaped them have once again made corporations preeminent.

Today's leading revolutionary force is not the state but the business corporation, turning the mechanical industrial age into the electronic age. Since 1980, corporation-produced miracles such as computers, word processors, fax machines, satellite transmissions, fiber optics, genetic research, and medicines heretofore unseen have transformed the world.

Under Democrats as well as Republicans, the great American job machine has continued to turn out more jobs, and higher-paying jobs, than this country has ever known: more than 50 million new jobs since 1970. Great experiments have also been launched (and already once or twice revised) in corporate structures, management reorganization, work groups, and internal entrepreneurship. Who today can doubt that the most dynamic institution in the world is the business corporation?

Thus, whatever new steps are still to be taken in reforming corporate governance, such steps must protect the inimitable creativity of the business corporation as a unique form of social organization. Its freedom and flexibility are the envy of other institutions. These must be protected, under any and all new schemes for reorganization. If this freedom and flexibility are not protected, the entire society will suffer. In periods of economic decline, the poor suffer most of all.

Only in periods of dynamism and creativity do ever greater numbers of the poor rise out of poverty and discover their own talents for accomplishment. In finding a route out of poverty, second only to small businesses, public corporations are the poor's best friend. That is the main reason why healthy business corporations are the sine qua non for the success of democracy.

Corporate leaders often lose sight of the fact that the most important secondary effect of what they do—not what they aim at, perhaps, but what their actions lead to—is to raise the poor out of poverty and to

offer unparalleled opportunities for the development
of human talents. Their further great effect is to ani-
mate civil society, that huge, bustling arena of the
world's grand experiment in self-government. These
two signal achievements, raising up the poor and
energizing civil society, provide powerful moral
claims for business corporations. Corporate leaders
should take care that new schemes for corporate governance do not jeopardize these achievements nor
distort their one main purpose: to create new wealth
for the whole society.

Notes

1. The most influential is Britain's Will Hutton, with his elastic concept of "stakeholding" (see note 12, below). A moderate statement among recent studies is *Ownership and Control: Rethinking Corporate Governance for the Twenty-first Century,* Margaret W. Blair (Washington, D.C.: Brookings Institution, 1995); more critical and deeper is *The Genius of American Corporate Law,* Roberta Romano (Washington, D.C.: AEI Press, 1993); a study by two leaders in the stakeholder movement is Robert A. G. Marks and Nell Minow, *Watching the Watchers: Corporate Governance for the 21st Century* (Cambridge, Mass.: Blackwell, 1996).

2. Adam Smith, *An Inquiry into the Nature and Causes of the Wealth of Nations,* vol. II, ed. R. H. Campbell and A. S. Skinner (Indianapolis, Ind.: Liberty Classics, 1981), p. 741.

3. As Karl Marx and Frederick Engels wrote: "The bourgeoisie, during its rule of scarce one hundred years, has created more massive and more colossal productive forces than have all preceding generations together. Subjection of Nature's forces to man, machinery, application of chemistry to industry and agriculture, steam-navigation, railways, electric telegraphs, clearing of whole continents for cultivation, canalization of rivers, whole populations conjured out of the ground—what earlier century had even a presentiment that such productive forces slumbered in the lap of social labor?" *The Communist Manifesto* (New York: International Publishers, 1948), pp. 13–14.

4. Of Japanese corporate life, Peter Drucker has written: "In Japan . . . the large employer—government agency or business—has increasingly attempted to become a 'community' for its employees. 'Lifetime employment' is only one

affirmation of this. Company housing, company health plans, company vacations, and so on, all emphasize for the Japanese employee that the employer, and especially the big corporation, is the community and the successor to yesterday's family."

But Drucker himself has noted the shift in Japan away from this idea in recent years, a result of the growing number of people who earn their living through brain-power: "The young knowledge people in Japan still sing the company song. They still expect the company to provide them job security. However, not only do they refuse, increasingly, to sacrifice their family life to the company, but they increasingly are as ready as their counterparts to change jobs if there is a better one available." *Managing in a Time of Great Change* (New York: Dutton, 1995), pp. 253–54.

Francis Fukuyama has also recently explored the changing corporate culture of Japan in his *Trust: The Social Virtues and the Creation of Prosperity* (New York: Free Press, 1995), pp. 161–93. See also Jonathan P. Charkhan, *Keeping Good Company: A Study of Corporate Governance in Five Countries* (Oxford: Clarendon Press, 1994), pp. 70–118, "Japan," esp. p. 71.

5. See Michael Oakeshott, *On Human Conduct* (Oxford: Oxford University Press, 1975). Oakeshott defines an enterprise association as "substantive; it is an association in co-operative 'doing.' And there may be as many such associations as there are purposes to invoke joint pursuit" (p. 315). A civil association, in contrast, is "formal; not in terms of the satisfaction of substantive wants but in terms of the conditions to be observed in seeking the satisfaction of wants" (p. 313). (For Oakeshott, government must be viewed as a civic association, that is, "formal" and "rule governed"; otherwise, it would be led to impose substantive ways of acting and being on free persons, thus denying their liberty.)

6. Irving Kristol led me to this insight: "You can't have 'separation of powers' within corporate leadership any more than you can have separation of powers within the executive branch of government." "What Is a CEO Worth?" *Wall Street Journal,* June 5, 1996.

7. As Alexander Hamilton wrote in *The Federalist Papers* (New York: New American Library, 1961) No. 70: "Energy in the executive is the leading character in the definition of good government. It is essential to the protection of the community against foreign attacks; it is not less essential to the steady administration of the laws; to the protection of property against those irregular and high-handed combinations which sometimes interrupt the ordinary cause of justice; to the security of liberty against the enterprises and assaults of ambition, of faction, and of anarchy" (p. 423).

8. See my *Choosing Our King: Powerful Symbols in Presidential Politics* (New York: Macmillan, 1974), recently reissued and expanded as *Choosing Presidents: Symbols of Political Leadership* (Rutgers, N.J.: Transaction, 1992), esp. part one, "Priest, Prophet, King," pp. 3–53.

9. On the functions of boards, see William G. Bowen, *Inside the Boardroom: Governance by Directors and Trustees* (New York: John Wiley & Sons, Inc., 1944), pp. 17–38. His list includes these: to select, encourage, and if necessary replace CEOs; to adopt long-term strategy; to ensure resources will match the strategy; to monitor management; and to nominate strong candidates for the board.

Persons with experience on corporate boards have stressed to me that boards have two chief general functions, which need to be finely balanced: first, to give counsel about upcoming decisions; second, to monitor ongoing structures, practices, and actions. Too much of one, to the neglect of the other, is a bad mistake. Respecting these two tendencies, the ideal board should be balanced, even temperamentally.

10. As Aristotle wrote, "Precision is not to be sought for alike in all discussions, any more than in all the products of the crafts . . . it is the mark of an educated man to look for precision in each class of things just so far as the nature of the subject admits." Nicomachean Ethics, bk. 1: chap. 2, 1094, in *The Basic Works of Aristotle*, ed. R. McKeon (New York: Random House, 1941), p. 936.

11. See, for example, Drucker's *The Concept of the Corporation* (New York: Harper & Row Library, 1946), chap. 2; and

Managing in a Time of Great Change: "With the emergence of the knowledge society, society has become a society of organizations. Most of us work in and for an organization, are dependent for our effectiveness and equally for our living on access to an organization, whether as an organization's employee or as provider of services to an organization—as a lawyer, for instance, or a freight forwarder. And more and more of these supporting services to organizations are, themselves, organized as organizations. The first law firm was organized in the United States a little over a century ago—until then lawyers practiced as individuals. In Europe there were no law firms to speak of until after World War II. Today, the practice of law is increasingly done in larger and larger partnerships. But that is also true, especially in the United States, of the practice of medicine. The knowledge society is a society of organizations in which practically every single social task is being performed in and through an organization"(p. 245).

12. As in Will Hutton's influential *The State We're In* (London: Vintage, 1996), which has had an effect on Tony Blair's vision of transforming England into a "stakeholder" society. For a powerful critique of Hutton and other advocates of Britain's New Labour, see David Willetts, *Blair's Gurus* (London: Centre for Policy Studies, 1996), esp. pp. 13–24. See also my *The Future of the Corporation* (Washington, D.C.: AEI Press, 1996), delivered as the first of the three Pfizer Lectures.

13. See David Brock's discussion of Hillary Rodham Clinton's path to statism, in *The Seduction of Hillary Rodham* (New York: Free Press, 1996), pp. 112–16.

14. It is a serious error, for example, for IBM to bow to the demands of activists and extend their health plans to pay for domestic partners of homosexual relationships. Domestic partners are not spouses; acts of sodomy—the distinguishing feature of gay relationships—are not morally equivalent to marital acts; and ceding such moral equivalence is a serious moral step not submitted to shareholders for their approval. IBM, in fact, extends spousal benefits *only* to homosexual couples, refusing to do so in the case of heterosexual

couples living together without being married. Nationwide, 313 companies, including Disney and Coors, have embraced spousal benefits for homosexual couples. See Norman Podhoretz, "How the Gay Rights Movement Won," *Commentary* (November 1996), pp. 32–41.

15. Witness the role played by certain corporations in the struggle against the 1996 CCRI, a ballot initiative that would end state-sponsored race and gender preferences throughout California. As Heather MacDonald writes: "The lovefest between the advocates and the corporate establishment depends partly on corporate self-interest. Businesses pay off the anti-discrimination machine in the hope of inoculating themselves against litigation. But the relationship has another basis as well: There exists inside corporations a parallel network of activists who share the same goals as, and maintain close contact with, the civil rights groups. This is the internal affirmative action apparatus, a fearsome bureaucracy that just grows and grows. Pacific Bell, for example, employs diversity managers, equal employment opportunity investigators, and affirmative action officers." "Why They Hate CCRI," *Weekly Standard* (October 28, 1996), p. 24.

16. See Novak, *The Future of the Corporation.*

17. As a survey of American business recently put it: "The American business scene has a clearly identifiable ethos. Where most other rich countries are devoted to continuity, America is devoted to change—or, as some of its businessmen are increasingly fond of saying, to 'creative destruction.' That makes it a unique laboratory, from which the whole world has something to learn." "Back on Top? A Survey of American Business," *Economist* (September 16, 1995), p. 4.

18. Even as late as 1899, there were only 207,514 business establishments across the entire United States, with an average number of twenty-three employees. See Charles Gide, *Principles of Political Economy,* trans. E. Row (Boston: D.C. Heath and Company, 1924), pp. 171–72.

19. For the *locus classicus* on the separation of ownership and management in the corporation, leading to a "managerial capitalism," see Adolf A. Berle and Gardiner C. Means,

The Modern Corporation on Private Property (New York: Harcourt, Brace & World, Inc., 1932).

20. Nobel laureate Coase summarized his view thus: "In my article on 'The Nature of the Firm' I argued that, although production could be carried out in a completely decentralized way by means of contracts between individuals, the fact that it costs something to enter into these transactions means that firms will emerge to organize what would otherwise be market transactions whenever their costs were less than the costs of carrying out the transactions through the market. The limit to the size of the firm is set where its costs of organizing a transaction become equal to the cost of carrying it out through the market. This determines what the firm buys, produces, and sells." R. H. Coase, *The Firm, the Market, and the Law* (Chicago: University of Chicago Press, 1988), p. 7. See also "The Nature of the Firm," pp. 33–56.

21. Posner succinctly summarizes his view in this way: "Contrast two methods of organizing production. In the first, the entrepreneur contracts with one person to supply the component parts, with another to assemble them, and with a third to sell the finished product. In the second, he hires them to perform these tasks as his employees under his direction . . . . The essence of the first method is that the entrepreneur negotiates with each of the three producers an agreement specifying the price, quantity, quality, delivery date, credit terms, and guarantees of the contractor's performance. The essence of the second method is that the entrepreneur pays the producers a wage—a price not for a specific performance but for the right to direct their performance. . . .

"In sum, the contract method of organizing economic activity encounters the problem of high transaction costs, the method of organizing economic activity through the firm, the problem of loss of control." Richard A. Posner, *The Economic Analysis of Law*, 4th ed. (Boston: Little Brown & Company, 1992), pp. 391–427, 391–92.

22. The actions of some unions have, to some degree, thrown this process into reverse. It has become more efficient and less time-consuming for some corporations to shed

certain operations, in favor of competitively priced suppliers.

23. On the "corporate raiders," Irwin Stelzer observes: "Many serious students of America's corporations, even those who were no fans of the so-called predators who mounted hostile takeovers in the 1980s, came to realize that something was not quite right with the way many large companies were being run. When Milken broke the commercial banks' monopoly of corporate credit by making it possible for non-establishment entrepreneurs (a.k.a. the 'predators') to raise money by selling high-yield bonds (disparagingly called 'junk' by the five percent of companies that until then were the only ones that could issue corporate debt, and by their generally 'white shoe' investment banking and law firms), he unleashed a new breed of entrepreneurs on over-manned and over-perked corporations. He also ameliorated what economists call the 'principal-agent problem.' That problem arises when the agent designated to act for a principal has incentives to behave in ways that are not in the interest of the principal he represents." "Are CEOs Overpaid?" *The Public Interest* (Winter 1997), p. 28.

24. Murray Weidenbaum, director of the Center for the Study of American Business, divides criticisms of corporate management into three categories: the board of directors is a "rubber stamp," consisting of an "old boy" network "that makes it personally unpleasant for directors to question the performance of their peers"; the board is dominated by the CEO (CEOs serve as chairman of the board in 80 percent of the larger corporations); and the board is plagued with conflicts of interest. See "The Evolving Corporate Board," *CSAB Contemporary Issues Series* 65 (May 1994), pp. 2–5.

25. Michael Useem observes the shifting pattern of corporate ownership: "In 1965, individual holdings constituted 84 percent of corporate stock, institutional holdings 16 percent. By 1990, the individual fraction had declined to 54 percent, and the institutional fraction had risen to 46 percent. A closer look at the 1,000 publicly traded companies with highest market value during the latter 1980s and 1990s reveals

much the same trend. Between 1985 and 1994 . . . the institutional share rose by more than a point a year, topping the 50
percent threshold in 1990 and reaching 57 percent by 1994."
*Investor Capitalism: How Money Managers Are Changing the Face
of Corporate America* (New York: Basic Books, 1996), p. 25.

26. Roberta Romano notes the growing proportion of
pension fund investment: "The percentage of corporate equity held by institutional investors generally, and by pension funds in particular, has increased exponentially over the
past few decades. From holding less than 1 percent in 1950,
pension funds held 26 percent of corporate equity by 1989.
Public pension funds are approximately 30 percent of this
sector." "The Politics of Public Pension Funds," *The Public
Interest* (Spring 1995), p. 44. Peter Drucker was one of the
first to notice this phenomenon in his *Unseen Revolution: How
Pension Fund Socialism Came to America* (New York: Harper &
Row, 1976).

27. See Michael P. Smith, "Shareholder Activism by Institutional Investors: Evidence from CalPERS," *Journal of Fi-
nance*, vol. 51, no. 1 (March 1996), pp. 227–52. As the socialist
writer Richard Mimms points out: "By 1994 the world-wide
accumulated assets of pension funds totalled $10,000 billion,
equivalent to the market value of all the companies quoted
on the world's three largest stock markets." "The Social
Ownership of Capital," *New Left Review*, vol. 219 (Septem-
ber/October 1996), p. 43.

28. As the U.S. Department of Labor itself says in its
1995 Report on the American Work Force: "Several types of statistics are available to indicate whether there have been shifting trends in job stability. These include data on job tenure,
retention rates, job turnover, and part-year work. All suggest that there has been little change in overall job stability."
Quoted in Karl Zinsmeister, "Indicators: Special Edition on
Economic Anxiety," *The American Enterprise* (July/August
1996), p. 18. This July/August number presents many reveal-
ing charts and figures. Among the most interesting are these
two:

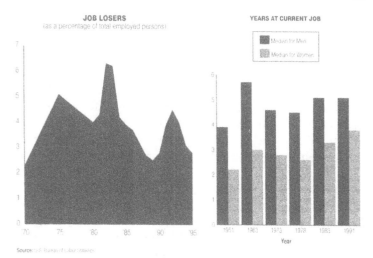

JOB LOSERS
(as a percentage of total employed persons)

YEARS AT CURRENT JOB

Median for Men
Median for Women

Source: U.S. Bureau of Labor Statistics

29. Amity Shlaes stresses that most treatments complaining about AT&T's 40,000 layoffs leave out the fact "that communications and computer services, a sector that includes AT&T, created 408,000 new American jobs in the last four years, growing at a robust 4.6%." "A National Case of the Jitters," *Wall Street Journal,* June 4, 1996.

30. The conventional wisdom is that most new jobs are created by small businesses. The source most often quoted is the Small Business Administration, but in reporting job growth by small businesses, the SBA concentrates on small businesses that succeed, and ignores those that fail. Thus *net* job growth from small businesses is far smaller than often described. A brief account of how and why the conventional view is wrong—and how and why most job growth occurs in businesses employing 500 or more people—is found in David Hirschberg, "Small-Biz Blarney: What Does It Take to Kill a Bad Number," *Slate,* posted October 17, 1997.

31. As "chainsaw" Al Dunlop says, "In my experience, the success of a company is inversely proportional to the size and opulence of the headquarters." Dunlop took over Scott Paper, a Fortune 500 conglomerate whose stock price was "in the basement" when it lost $277 million dollars in 1993. A

bloated corporate staff was spending over $30 million a year on consultants and corporate perks. After two years of restructuring, sell-offs, and "shock therapy," Dunlop had virtually eliminated Scott's $2.5 billion of debt and had increased the value of the company's shares from $2.5 billion in 1993 to $9 billion as of last year. Richard Miniter suggests that Dunlop did this by bringing "focus and energy to the executive suite" in "Al Dunlop and the Shareholder Revolution," *The American Enterprise* (November/December 1996), pp. 82–83.

32. According to Stelzer, "The chore of explaining and defending executive compensation is being made more difficult than need be by some corporate governance practices in need of reexamination. In many cases such compensation is set by board members who are themselves CEOs of other companies, who are often selected by the executives whose salaries they are to determine, and who are treated by those executives to a variety of 'perks,' ranging from use of the corporate jet to special pensions. When these board members convene to decide just how much to pay the company's chief executive officer, it is not seen by outsiders as a meeting of hard-nosed performance appraisers. And when they are assisted in their deliberations by compensation consultants who are also looking to the CEO for fee-rich assignments setting up company-wide benefits plans, the problem is compounded. And when corporate executives resist efforts by the regulators to have them reveal the estimated value of options they receive, and refuse to charge the present value of that sum against current earnings, suspicions that this may not be the most honest game in town understandably mount." "The Role and Governance of the Corporation," remarks delivered at the American Enterprise Institute's World Forum, June 22, 1996.

33. See "Business Should Act for All Its Stakeholders Before the Feds Do," *The CEO Series*, no. 9 (October 1996), pp. 5-7. I keep the author anonymous because, despite the glaring fault I am pointing out, his record as a corporate leader shows unusual courage and vigor in public argument. In this particular lecture, moreover, he deliberately selected an ar-

gument that (he judged) would persuade others in business, who are not as tuned in on the substance of the issues as he is. The fact that he felt an argument from appeasement might be more likely of success, than simply laying out the challenge, sadly confirms the strength of the habit of appeasement.

34. Stuart Nolan, *Patterns of Corporate Philanthropy: Public Affairs Giving and the Forbes 250,* preface by Malcolm S. Forbes, Jr. (Washington, D.C.: Capital Research Center, 1994). This study should be taken as indicative, not probative, since corporate giving patterns are often closely held secrets. The actual records of some firms may be "better"—or "worse"—than the public materials available for this study suggest. Still, critics agree that while its reports on individual companies are unreliable because of the veil of secrecy, the study's general point is supported by a study of the actual funding received by antibusiness institutions. By law, these funding sources are made public in annual reports.

About the Author

MICHAEL NOVAK holds the George Frederick Jewett Chair in Religion, Philosophy, and Public Policy at the American Enterprise Institute. He is also AEI's director of social and political studies. In 1986, Mr. Novak headed the U.S. delegation to the Conference on Security and Cooperation in Europe. In 1981 and 1982, he led the U.S. delegation to the United Nations Human Rights Commission in Geneva. Mr. Novak has won the Templeton Prize for Progress in Religion, the Anthony Fisher Award, the Wilhelm Weber Prize, and the International Award of the Institution for World Capitalism, among others. The author of more than twenty-five books, he is also a cofounder and former publisher of *Crisis* and has been a columnist for both *National Review* and *Forbes*; he is now a regular contributor to *USA Today*.